Life Cycle of a

Chicken

Angela Royston

Heinemann
LIBRARY

First published in Great Britain by Heinemann Library
Halley Court, Jordan Hill, Oxford OX2 8EJ,
a division of Reed Educational and Professional Publishing Ltd.

Heinemann is a registered trademark of Reed Educational and Professional
Publishing Limited.

Oxford Melbourne Auckland Kuala Lumpur Singapore
Ibadan Nairobi Kampala Johannesburg Gaborone
Portsmouth NH (USA) Chicago

Designed by Celia Floyd
Illustrations by Alan Fraser
Printed in Hong Kong / China

03 02 01 00 99
10 9 8 7 6 5 4 3 2 1

ISBN 0 431 08376 2
This title is also available in a hardback edition (ISBN 0 431 08367 3)

British Library Cataloguing in Publication Data

Royston, Angela
Life cycle of a chicken
1. Chickens – Juvenile literature
I. Title II. Chicken
598.6'25

Acknowledgements
The Publisher would like to thank the following for permission to reproduce
photographs:
Bruce Coleman Ltd/Jane Burton pgs 9, 12; Heather Angel pg 8; NHPA/William
Paton pg 24, NHPA/Manfred Danegger pg 25; Oxford Scientific Films/David
Thompson pg 11, Oxford Scientific Films/Michael Leach pg 13, Oxford Scientific
Films/G I Bernard pgs 26-27; Photo Researchers Inc/Tim Davis pg 10, Photo
Researchers Inc/Kenneth H Thomas pgs 14, 23; Roger Scruton pgs 4, 5, 6, 7, 15, 16,
17, 18, 19, 20, 21, 22.

Cover photograph: Britstock-IFA/Bernd Ducke.

Our thanks to Dr Bryan Howard, University of Sheffield, for his comments in the
preparation of this edition.

Contents

Meet the chickens

Chickens are birds. They have feathers, wings and a **beak**. Different kinds of chickens have different coloured feathers.

Egg

3 weeks

I day old

The chicken in this book is a White Leghorn cockerel. He began life inside an egg. The egg was laid by his mother, a White Leghorn hen.

7 weeks

1 year

The eggs are laid

The mother hen laid the egg in a nest. Every day she lays another egg and now there are six eggs in the nest.

Egg

3 weeks

I day old

The mother hen sits on the eggs to keep them warm. Inside each egg a new chick is growing.

7 weeks

1 year

3 weeks later

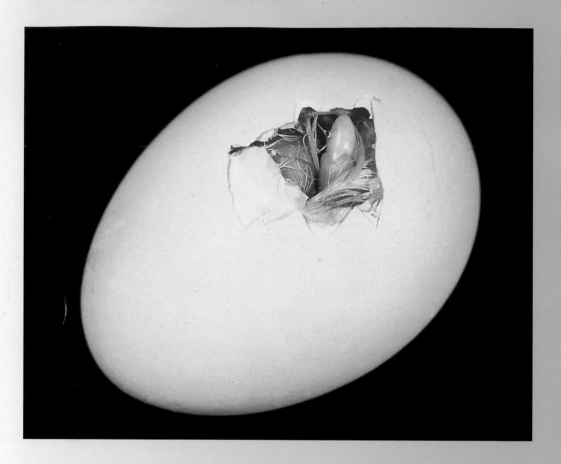

The mother hen hears a tiny tapping sound. The eggs are beginning to **hatch**. The chick uses its **beak** to chip a hole in the shell.

Egg

3 weeks

I day old

It chips a hole all around the egg. Now it uses its body to push the egg apart. The little chick is wet and tired.

7 weeks

1 year

I day old

Very soon its soft, **downy** feathers have dried. The little chick stands up and looks around.

Egg

3 weeks

I day old

This chick has just **hatched** too.
Soon all the chicks have left the
eggs and are cheeping loudly.

7 weeks

1 year

4 days old

The little chicks drink water and peck seeds in the straw. They stay close together and follow the mother hen wherever she goes.

Egg

3 weeks

I day old

This chick has been left behind! He is scared and lonely. Then he hears his mother clucking and he runs after her.

7 weeks

1 year

7 weeks old

The chicks are bigger now, but they still shelter under their mother's wing. New, white feathers have grown in place of the yellow **down**.

Egg

3 weeks

1 day old

This young cockerel is very proud of his long tail feathers and the red **comb** on top of his head.

7 weeks

1 year

2 months

The chickens leave their mother and live in the **chicken run** with the other hens. Here the cockerel has flown up onto the fence to have a look around.

Egg

3 weeks

1 day old

Now he pecks in the grass looking for seeds and worms. He swallows his food whole and it is ground up in a stomach called a **gizzard**.

7 weeks

I year

5 months

The chickens are nearly full grown. One day this hen sits in one of the egg boxes in the hen house. She clucks loudly and then climbs out.

18

Egg

3 weeks

I day old

She has just laid her first egg! From now on she will lay an egg almost every day. Her eggs have not been **fertilized**, so there are no chicks growing inside them.

7 weeks

1 year

8 months

The young cockerel struts around the farmyard. He watches carefully over several young hens. If one wanders off, he chases it back.

Egg

3 weeks

1 day old

The cockerel thinks these hens are his. If another cockerel comes near one of them, he chases it away.

7 weeks

I year

I year

This hen is ready to **mate**. The young cockerel mates with her and **fertilizes** her eggs. She lays the eggs and sits on them.

Egg

3 weeks

I day old

The eggs have **hatched** and there
is a new **brood** of chicks. The hen
looks after them, but the cockerel
keeps a close eye on them too.

7 weeks

I year

Danger!

Very early one morning a fox climbs into the **chicken run**. He is looking for a chicken to steal and eat. At first the chickens do not see him.

Egg

3 weeks

I day old

Then the fox grabs a hen. The cockerel and the other chickens squawk and flap, but the fox jumps out of the run and runs away.

7 weeks

1 year

The farmyard

The cockerel has a busy life. He watches over the hens and chicks and from time to time he crows loudly.

He will stay on the farm until he
dies. If the fox doesn't catch him,
he may live until he is about ten
years old.

Life cycle

Eggs

3 weeks later

1 day old

7 weeks old

1 year old

Fact file

A hen lays between 100 and 300 eggs a year, but not more than one a day.

The shell forms around the egg inside the hen's body. It takes about a day for the egg to form before it is ready to be laid.

People have kept chickens for over 3000 years. They collect their eggs and eat them.

Chickens are probably the most common bird in the world. There are more than 10 billion (10,000,000,000) of them.

Glossary

beak hard covering of a bird's mouth

brood a group of birds that hatch at the same time

chicken run an area of fenced-in ground near a hen house

comb a fleshy red crest on the top of a chicken's head

down soft feathers

fertilizes a female egg is fertilized when it joins with a sperm from a male

gizzard a special stomach for grinding up food before it passes into the chicken's second stomach

hatch to break out of an egg

mate when a male and a female come together to produce young

Index